MW01065035

A Casualty of Love

Stories of a Journey

Arjuna Kumar

PUBLISHED IN THE UNITED STATES OF AMERICA
BY
BLACK FOREST PRESS
P.O.Box 6342
Chula Vista, CA 91909-6342
1-800-451-9404

**Cover Design
by
Dale and Penni Neely**

Disclaimer

This document is an original work of the author. It may include reference to information commonly known or freely available to the general public. Any resemblance to other published information is purely coincidental. The author has in no way attempted to use material not of his own origination. Black Forest Press disclaims any association with or responsibility for the ideas, opinions or facts as expressed by the author of this book.

Printed in the United States of America
Library of Congress
Cataloging-in-Publication

ISBN: 1-58275-024-6

This book is dedicated to my niece Mariah, who saved my life without even knowing it.

And to my mother who has always been there for me.

Special Thanks

Since I have written this story, I have been trying to stay on the path. I have slipped a few times, but have not fallen. I owe my continuous recovery to those that mean the most to me. My friends have kept my head on straight and have taught me many more lessons about humanity.

I would like to express my utmost gratitude to those that have influenced me since my downward spiral. Bob and Nicole Long, who accept me for who I am and support me in whatever I have done. Mariah and Mercedez Long, Bob and Nicole's daughters who call me "Uncle". Darren and Pamela Martin, fast friends that lend an ear and emotional support, with straight-laced advice. Andy Shelley, friends since childhood that pick up wherever we leave off. Vynnette Frederick, a long distance friend who lent me an ear and speaks her mind. Shea Brackin, the first to read and give me feedback on "Casualty of Love", understanding where I was coming from and not pushing too hard. Mariah Morales, a woman of many talents, who supported me through my last year of school, and brought happiness back into my life. Kerry Hughes, a wonderful woman in my life who restored my confidence. My Mom, who loves me no matter what and supports everything I do, no matter how crazy. And especially Erica Gomez, a woman who taught me more than she knows. Who brought sunshine back into a heart that was dark and cold. She renewed the vigor of life that has always been there. I will be forever grateful.

Thank you my friends.
With love forever,
Your Friend.

What's in These Pages?

Well, here I am, back where I started, by myself with stories to tell. Everybody has stories, but these stories share a three month roller coaster ride, and what a ride it was. Some stories are short and others long. Some are funny and some are sad. I wrote these stories as I traveled through self-exploration, realization, love and life.

I will warn you now that you may feel lost and confused while reading these pages, but that's how I was while living and writing them. Don't worry though; by the time you reach the end you will know where I was, where I went, and where I am now. Maybe this will help you. Maybe you will learn to see the world and people differently, or maybe you will not. Anyway everybody has stories, and this collection is mine.

A Little Background

When I was a freshman in college I met a very beautiful girl. Soon after meeting her we became really close. She was my best friend and knew more about me than anyone ever had, I trusted her completely. A few months after meeting we became romantically involved and were together as lovers for a little over a year. Then on Valentines Day she came to me and told me there was another guy and she was leaving me, not wanting to see me again. I was shocked, completely surprised, and devastated. This event started everything that is written in these pages.

The Flower

As I walk through life my legs grow tired. I notice a quiet place to rest my weary body for a while. I sit down, my body collapsing in front of a pile of rubble and garbage, the pile no longer resembling its original form. I sit contemplating what life is all about. I just stare at what seems to be nothing, discarded refuse, my mind drifting.

Soon I notice a small green leaf growing where it shouldn't, where nothing should. The sun shines down on the leaf, giving it warmth. A while later the rain comes, nourishing the leaf. The leaf stretches out towards the sun, soon supported by a green stem. More rain falls, providing more nourishment. The sun provides the warmth and energy for the leaf to grow a bud and reach for the sun. I stay and observe, wondering about life, my life. Soon the bud opens and a beautiful purple flower bursts forth into the world. I know the flower. I have seen it before. I know how it moves in the breeze, sun and rain. I watch it grow from nothing, out of a pile of rubble, discarded rubbish. I look at the flower closely, observing everything.

Then I stepped back, to observe it from afar. I saw something beautiful growing out of nothing. I stepped further back and even further. The whole world was something beautiful growing out of nothing. I see my friend and love for her come out of nothing, discarded rubbish and garbage.

Before I met you I was nothing, alone, with a darkened heart. I kept to myself, promising myself that I would not meet anyone or fall in love. I did not want a relationship. I wanted to be alone and only alone. Then I met you, a beautiful flower.

You struck me and changed my life from the beginning. We grew together and you taught me how to love. We had good times, and great times. I loved just being in the same room with you, hearing your voice during our late-night chats. I loved holding you, feeling your caresses. I loved caressing you. You lit a fire in me, one that had been extinguished long ago. I loved you. Then you went away.

Now there are days that are good and most that aren't. I ache for the love that once engulfed me and filled my days. I opened up to you, you knew more about me than anyone else, even myself. You brought me out of my shell of protection. Where there was once nothing, you showed me how to love. I was happy, truly happy, for the first time since I was a child. You taught me how to hold and hug someone. Then you took it away. You took everything away.

Now I question everything. Everything you taught me and everything I trusted or believed is suspect. Now, I don't think it was worth it. Was it? I don't know anymore. You crushed me like a bug. You took everything I gave, all of me, everything precious, and destroyed it, throwing it out like garbage. I am now a pile of rubbish, back the way I was before I met you.

Confession of a Suicide

Where it all Began

I am a twenty-five year old white male. On my brother's twenty-eighth birthday I attempted to kill myself. Before I get into what I actually did, I want to tell you how I came to the position of committing suicide. So let's go back to where it all began.

When I was in the eighth grade my family moved from Walla Walla, Washington to Oregon City, Oregon. I lived for about thirteen years in Walla Walla and knew a lot of people, many I still know today. After moving I became extremely depressed. I hated changing where I lived and losing my friends. Though I put up a calm, cool front at school, I wanted to run away. Then during the fall of my freshman year I went with my parents to visit friends and family in Walla Walla.

I went out with my closest friends, and we were drinking and having a good time. Unfortunately, one of my friends had to go home from the party. When he got home and stumbled into the bathroom, his mom confronted him about being drunk. He confessed and told her everything. She was a friend of my moms, so of course she called and told her everything. Drunker than a skunk, I was busted for the first time ever. My depression got worse and I began to have terrible nightmares. Buried emotions began to surface. I finally cried for my aunt who had passed away about five years earlier and told my mom how I felt. She promised she would try and help as soon as we got back to Oregon City. I was relieved and hopeful about getting help and getting on with my life.

When we got home I did go and see a psychiatrist one time. However I decided that I wanted to forget the past and get on with my new life. I had succeeded at changing and adapting. I started to write and had found that writing was a release for me. I began to believe that I had some great potential!

We lived in Oregon City for two years before we moved to North Bend, Oregon. I was happy to get away from the suburb of Portland! The first summer I was in North Bend I got a job, at McDonald's! It was great to have a job and I even made the varsity soccer team. Soccer was my life and my first love. and I had been playing since the second grade. However at the end of my junior year I injured my knee. Believing my soccer career was over, I turned to the typical wrong crowd. I started drinking, staying out, skipping school, and just plain not caring anymore. In the spring I tried out for track, feeling and hoping my knee was better. Soon after beginning practice I learned my knee was actually worse. I had to have surgery to remove some cartilage. I hit another low. After surgery I truly believed my soccer career was over, and I lost part of my love for the game. That summer I asked my parents if I could move back to Walla Walla and graduate from high school with my friends. They agreed, and off I went, to live with my grandmother.

I was extremely happy to be back in Walla Walla. However I quickly learned that most people had forgotten me and that since the soccer season was in the spring, I wouldn't be playing. I got a job working with my friend, washing dishes at an Italian cafe. I signed up to join the Coast Guard soon after, departing in June. My friends and I partied all the time. I was drunk at least five days a week, if not more. I was also getting laid! I was on cloud nine! I couldn't think of a better life. With all the partying I began to skip classes and not bother to do homework! During the winter, just before break, I collapsed at school and had to be taken to the hospital. To this day I have no idea why. I just know I was sick. The whole incident scared me. I decided to go back to North Bend to live with my parents. When I went to enroll in school I was told that I would fail one of my classes from Walla Walla, due, of course, to my partying. I was told I had to make up the class in the summer. It was a required course, but I couldn't make the class up because I was leaving for the Coast Guard in June. I was not shocked or devastated. I kind of knew it was coming, and when my mom suggested I get my GED, I decided to do that. I got my GED in March and began the wait for my departure date for basic training.

Soon after receiving my GED I got a letter in the mail asking me to play soccer in Europe and watch a World Cup game! The only thing I needed to do was pay $1800. I borrowed the money from my Grandparents and went to Europe. I had a blast, playing the sport I loved, for the last time, in the place where soccer is king. I gave it everything I had. The day I came back from Europe, I left for basic training. After two months of training I was stationed on a cutter in Guam.

At first Guam was fun, exciting, exotic, and new. I traveled to and saw many small islands, including the Philippines, and Palau. However things changed quickly, as I felt isolated from the world and from my family. In January I flew home to be with my mom as my stepfather underwent heart bypass surgery. The surgery was successful and I liked being back home. I was home for twenty days before going back to Guam.

The boat was out so I was pretty much by myself. The first night back I drank until I passed out, then drank some more. I puked and eventually fell off my bed, from a height of six feet, face first onto a cement floor. The fall left me two scars, one above my left eye, the other across the bridge of my nose. I thought I was going to die that night and wished I would. I had sunk emotionally to a new low!

A week later the boat came back and I drank even more. I was drunk at work, at home, and every time I can remember. Soon after my nineteenth birthday, celebrated alone, I stopped drinking and started thinking of my future, but three months later my future seemed to be over. There was a change in leadership within my department. They wanted us to tell them what religious affiliation we were because a priest was coming on board. I told them the truth, that I was an atheist. From that day my immediate superiors began to single me out. While we were in Saipan, and I was sick, I was ordered to go out and work while everybody else got to play or sleep. When one of my supervisors told me that I didn't have to, his junior superior began to cuss and yank me from my bed. I told him to go fuck himself. The next thing I knew I was being investigated for insubordination. I was found guilty and sentenced to extra duty for ten days and no chance of promotion for six months. The next day, I later learned, I received orders to leave the boat for schooling.

For the rest of the time we were on the Philippines I drank every night and did whatever I wanted to whom ever I wanted. Every day I was drunk while I was working, firing machine guns, lowering boats, and doing whatever I was told. On the way back to Guam I wanted to jump off the back of the boat and just float away. I wanted to see the name, Basswood, fading into the distance.

In October we were headed to Bellingham, Washington for repairs. I felt relieved because I was getting closer to home. The long trip, over thirty days, and the small boat, 180 feet, made me feel like a caged animal. I was extremely depressed and lonely. I didn't want to move from my bed, but I did. I got up everyday, stood my watch, and attempted to do the menial tasks I was assigned to keep busy. I even went out on deck, looking over the stern, wanting to escape. As the days grew colder, my activity grew less. When I wasn't on watch I was sleeping somewhere. When we finally made it to Seattle, my mood changed very little. I was still on the boat that I hated. Two days later when we were in Bellingham, I still wasn't happy.

My job, watching for fires on a boat that had nothing flammable on it, seemed meaningless. I wasn't having fun. I began to drink, which became monotonous. I was hung over at work, sometimes still drunk. I began to make up some games to play in order to make drinking more fun. I would go to Canada to get smashed. I was either defiant or stoic. I either had no emotions at all or hate consumed me. I couldn't stand where I was.

Within four months, which seemed like forever, I finally got my wish. I was transferred home. I was going to make a whole new career out of the Coast Guard. Since I was home again I stopped drinking and began to enjoy my life.I got to go to the America's Cup Yacht Race in San Diego. I was feeling good because I was finally doing things I always wanted to do. I was having fun and really liked my job and began thinking of advancing and making a career out of the Coast Guard. I even started seeing a girl named Kysha steadily.

I was happy and falling in love with someone for the first time. Things couldn't have been better. Then suddenly I I was told I was being charged with dereliction of duty. Somebody on the boat called 1-900 sex numbers on my watch, while in Portland, Oregon. I was told I was supposed to monitor the phone, all incoming and outgoing phone calls, which nobody did. I was found guilty because the Coast Guard needed to make an example out of somebody and hold someone responsible.

This time I was restricted to the boat for ten days, assigned extra duty for those days, and prevented from advancing for six months. Once again I felt my career was over. I decided I'd go to college and forget the Coast Guard.

Later that year after I was 21, I broke up with Kysha. We had grown apart, and I was devastated and alone again. I wanted to work things out but didn't know how. She moved on quickly by finding someone else to spend time with. I haven't talked to her since.

I had no time to talk to her because the boat left soon after to go on patrol. We were in rough seas and seasickness hit everybody. Not only was my heart crushed, I was also being thrown around like a rag doll. I wanted it to end, all of it. I had wished the boat would sink or that I would be accidentally thrown overboard. I didn't want to continue. I became what I was in Guam.

I began drinking, partying, and just doing my job, nothing extra. I did exactly what I was told without an emotion showing. I hated life and all there was to it. I was biding my time until I was discharged. Later I made up injuries to get off the boat. I didn't want to be in the Coast Guard, I didn't even want to see a uniform. I promised myself that I would not get emotionally attached to anybody ever again. My attitude was that no one else really mattered.

Finally, I was discharged in May. I was looking forward to putting my past behind me. I began to forget about the Coast Guard. I got a job in a warehouse, as a lowly stock boy. But that didn't last long. I moved up quickly. Within nine months I was running the warehouse, as a supervisor. I was making money and partying the nights away, having a great time doing both. I even began to take some classes, at a local community college. I was on the lookout for something better, always looking for a bigger piece of the pie. I even tried out for the soccer team at the college I was attending. I didn't make the team; this was the end of my career, officially. I knew soccer was gone when I joined the Coast Guard, but needed one more attempt to confirm it. My life had no one in it, just me, only me, I didn't care or want to care for anyone else except for a few friends I had known my entire life.

I was soon offered a job promotion to Seattle from Portland. It would have included more money and more opportunities. I jumped at the chance but soon after moving to a suburb of Seattle I became very lonely. I didn't like my new job. I was more of an assistant, so it was a demotion from what I had been doing. I dropped out of school, showed up late to work and slept all day. I also learned that my step dad had become severely ill. I wanted to go home, back to Portland. I was no longer having fun. I felt like a drone just plugging away at a pile of endless tasks. I even thought of killing myself, I felt like I had failed. I quit work and continued drinking. Soon my money ran out, my truck was repossessed and I moved back to Portland.

After moving into my parents' home I applied to Oregon State University and looked for work, while gaining my Oregon residency. Eventually I got a job working where my mom worked and began to pay off my enormous debt. Things began to look up as I had been accepted to Oregon State. I was working to pay off bills and knew I wouldn't be there long. I kept my distance from everybody. I was afraid to become attached in any way to anybody. In December when my stepfather passed away I was lucky enough to be around my mom as we both worked through our loss. A few months later I was verbally attacked at work and asked that something be done about it. Nothing was, so I left with the understanding that I would receive unemployment benefits. I soon learned that I wouldn't, and I had to go to court to get any. I won and lost at the same time. I got some money, which paid off a lot of debt, but I also lost money to the state. I was unemployed and looking forward to going to school in the fall.

Fall term came around, I moved into the dorms, and began studying, and drinking responsibly. The beginning of my first term was nothing special. However, towards the end of the term I met a girl. This girl, Sarika, took my breath away. I had to get to know her.

Winter term started out well and got even better. I found out that Sarika was in a lecture and lab of mine, so I had the opportunity to talk to her. We grew close and I fell in love. I spent as much time as I could with her, talking about everything. She started me on my quest for religion and my own philosophy of life. She opened up something in me that had been dead for long time. Just thinking about her brought warmth to my heart. After winter term I had moved out of the dorms and into my own apartment. Spring term was more of the same with Sarika, most of the time spent at my house. I was happy, happier than I've ever been. Unfortunately the summer break came and she went home for four months. Those months were long and hard, but my love grew, and so did hers. In the fall term she came back and life was good, again. I felt comfortable in every aspect of my life. I knew what I wanted for the first time in my life.

Winter term started out normal and happy, but soon took a turn for the worse. On Valentines Day, Sarika told me there was another guy. She'd only known him a few days but she was already sleeping with him. I was devastated. My life as I knew it was over. It seemed my heart was ripped from my chest and held in front of me. The pain was unbearable. How could she betray me like this? I hit the lowest point of my entire life. That night I planned to kill myself. However I still had hope. I loved her more than anything. I forgave her. But she was so cold that two agonizing days later I attempted to end my life.

The Attempt

I was really tired on the 16th, of February. I slept through my first class, and raced through the midterm of my second. Then I went home to sleep. Sarika came over around four and we said goodbye. I knew what I was going to do. She had one last chance to stop me, but didn't. My heart and soul were crushed. I felt like a failure who couldn't do anything right. I had lost my world when Sarika said goodbye. I felt like there was nothing else to live for. The comfort, joy and love I knew were gone, replaced with pain. I wanted to hurt her as much as she hurt me. The only thing I could think of was to take me away. I wanted the pain to stop.

I began to think of life without her, and I couldn't handle it. I couldn't live without the love of my life, the one woman who made my world turn. She was the sunlight in my life. How can a person live without sunlight? I couldn't. So I moved my plan to commit suicide up by one day, and went about my task.

I wrote my mom, Sarika, and Chuck. I described what I wanted when I was dead. I began to drink, to numb the pain. Chuck left, and I went about the task of killing myself. I got a couple of knives and the liquor I was drinking. I gulped one last swallow and drew a bath. I sent the e-mails to mom and Sarika.

I climbed into the bathtub and began to cut my left wrist. The knives I had were too dull to penetrate my skin. I quickly got out of the tub, drank some more and found a razor blade. I mixed some liquid plumber with the alcohol and gulped it down. Then I mixed the liquid plumber with water and took a swallow. I climbed back into the tub and began again.

The blade was sharp and cut rather quickly at first. I saw a little blood and continued to open the cut. I tried to find the vein, but couldn't. I eventually had a good flow of blood streaming from my left wrist. The hot water was supposed to keep it flowing. I decided to open another vein. I was getting really tired, probably from the alcohol.

I moved to the crook of my elbow and opened another cut. I couldn't hit a vein, as I had wanted. I was growing more tired. The blood flow was like a stream, just pumping out with every heartbeat. I felt like the blood leaving my body was carrying my feelings for Sarika. As the blood streamed out of my wrist, my feelings for her went with it. I moved to my right wrist, but could barely penetrate the skin. Just as I was trying Chuck came home and found me. I was still alive!

He asked me if this was going to solve anything. I said yes and told him to go away. He said he was calling the paramedics and left the bathroom. I felt angry, because I wasn't dead. I was angry with Chuck for finding me. I just wanted to die. Soon I felt someone yelling at me and slapping my face. I was semi-conscious. I heard them asking me why I did this. I felt them drain the tub. I heard them say my wounds were superficial, that my blood coagulated. I had stopped bleeding naturally. They wrapped my cuts and hauled me out of the tub. They asked if I took anything, like drugs or something. I said no. I wanted to be dead, not being hauled away. As I lay on the stretcher I told them I drank something liquid from under the sink. They found the liquid plumber.

Lying in the ambulance, I was mad and didn't want to co-operate. The paramedics were treating me like the animal I thought I was. I wasn't human. I didn't want to be human. I wanted to be dead. They jabbed needles into my arms trying to find a vein for the I.V. The third time was the charm. I was cold, tired and mad. I answered their questions about me, not about why I did it. I didn't want to be there but I was and off we went to the hospital.

The Hospital

I was transferred to another stretcher as soon as I got to the Hospital. Monitors were attached to my finger for pulse, my chest for heart rate, and my right arm for blood pressure. I was asked over and over why I did it. I just said, "Because." I was extremely cold and was left alone. There was a security guard positioned outside the door. I kept wondering how could I do this to myself, how I got to this point. I felt the pain in my arm where the cuts were.

After at least an hour the doctor finally came in to put stitches in my arm. He numbed the areas and began to sew the cuts closed. I felt the tug of the skin and the pain of a couple of stitches. I answered his questions rudely and without emotion. I still couldn't believe I cut myself, until the pain in my arm finally hit me. I kept thinking that God must have stopped the bleeding, and that something more powerful than I was, did believe in me, and that my life mattered. After the doctor was done he told me a person from mental health was coming to talk to me.

I turned to my right and a guy introduced himself as being from county mental health. He began by asking me how I got to where I was. I told him I didn't know. A rush of emotions swept over me, from hatred, to joy, to anger, to happiness, to sadness. I didn't know who I was or what I was doing. I had lost it. I answered his questions with reluctance and downright rudeness. He wanted to put me on drugs for depression. I told him no. I kept wondering how I was going to face any of my friends or family. I was ashamed of what I had done.

After the psychiatrist left I was left alone for what seemed an eternity. I had just my thoughts. I thought that if I had waited for one day I would be dead, it would have been too late for anyone to find me. I thought about buying a gun and finishing the job. I thought about my lifelong friends. I thought about my family. I thought about my future. What it would be like? What would I lose? But most of all I thought about God. I thought that God, my God, saved my life. He stopped the bleeding. He must love me for who I am. He must believe in me for me. God saved my life. What a revelation! I was at peace when I was thinking that my God had saved my life.

Eventually my tranquility was broken when my brother came in. He just started to cry. I didn't want him to cry, not for me. I held back my tears as best I could. I didn't want to see him. I was ashamed for what I had done. I felt dirty. I had hurt more people than I wanted to. I only wanted to hurt one. Soon the mental health worker asked to talk to my brother.

About a half an hour later I saw my brother walk down the hall. He didn't even look at me. I knew I was definitely going to the mental health unit. The nurse came in and started disconnecting everything. She told me I was going to the unit on a five-day legal hold. I said nope! I didn't want to go. I wanted to go home. I wanted to run away. I wanted to leave this place. She summoned the security guard and off I went, upstairs to the mental ward.

When I got up there I answered their questions, was assigned a room and let loose to do what I wanted within the confines of the locked unit. The first thing I did after going to the bathroom was call Chuck and apologize. As I was talking to him my mom called. I talked to her for about three minutes, then went to try to sleep. I couldn't. So I got up and went to watch TV. I wasn't interested. So I sat in the hall until I felt a little tired. Finally I went to bed to relax and meditate. For the first time in over a month I could meditate. I fell asleep.

Meditation used to be a big thing in my life. The next day I stayed in my room. I meditated the entire morning. Just before noon the doctor came in to talk to me. I answered all his questions with honesty. He told me he wanted to talk to my mom and brother and that if their stories jibed with mine then I could be let go that day. So I went back to my room to be alone, and waited.

As I sat staring at nothing, or lying with my eyes closed, I thought about what I was going to tell people, especially my friends. I also thought about getting a gun when I got out. I thought I would take the gun, go to Sarika, put the gun in my mouth and pull the trigger in front of her. I also thought of how I was going to get on with my life. How desperately I wanted out of the hospital and to get on with my life. I felt like a trapped animal. I wanted to escape. I thought of breaking the window and climbing out. I thought of how I could get past the nurses, the locked outer doors and out of the hospital.

Later that night I finally paged my mom and talked to her about getting out. No one would give me answers. No one would give her answers. I was frustrated and angry. I called Chuck at home and asked if he would bring me some clothes. Later that evening he did. I had no one else visit or call. I thought about what I would tell the doctor the next day. I was told that my mom and I were to meet with him at 9:00 the next morning. I couldn't sleep that night either. I tossed and turned, my thoughts racing.

The next day, the 18th, I finally met the doctor around 11:00. Until that time I had no idea what was going on. I learned my mom had seen the doctor that morning and gave him a piece of her mind. He called security on her and probably wanted her admitted to the mental ward. I told him a great fat lie! I told him that I had lost God and had found him again; that I knew what I did was wrong and didn't want to do it again. Then I started talking about things he admitted to not comprehending, about world religions and studies. He told me to talk to a professor at school he knew and maybe the professor would understand what I was talking about, because he didn't.

Eventually, the doctor told me that I would have to see someone from the county mental health and, if that person said I was free to go, then I could go. So I sat in my room until the county guy showed up around 3:00. I pretty much told him the same thing about giving up on God and then finding him again, and that my goal in life was to prove there is only one religion. I also told him I could get over Sarika. He believed my story and let me go. I was home a little after 6:00 that night.

Facing the World

The night of the 18th, my mom took me home. Chuck was home and his mom was there, going over taxes. I saw boxes of things and some stuff of his was gone. I checked my e-mail and wrote Sarika to tell her I was home. I took a shower and talked to my mom for a while. Then I talked to my roommate, who told me he had given notice and was moving out, without me. I just said okay. I went into the living room, told my mom, and started thinking about what I was going to do. I wanted to study for my class the next day. Once my mom left that is what I did.

Then Sarika called. I didn't want to talk to her, as least not on the phone. She came over and we talked, hugged and cried. She'd disturbed me and shaken me to my core once again. She knew me so well, too well. She went to leave. I didn't want her to. She asked if I wanted to stay with her that night. I said, "yes," and we went to her place. She said she had to study with one of her friends and would be back around midnight. I said okay. I started to lie down, but my mind was racing. I found her journal, read some entries and became furious over her total disregard for me. She had sex with him the day she came over and told me she was seeing someone else. She said she didn't feel guilty about it either. I called her at her new "man's" house. Then I called her mom, and walked home. I was flying high. I felt good. I got home and called her mom again, and gave her the number where Sarika was. I was feeling even better. I got a phone call from Sarika and she began asking why. Then some guy got on the phone yelling at me and threatening to kill me, and kick my ass if he ever saw me on campus. I felt good. I screwed up her life like she screwed up mine, so I thought.

Chuck came home and I told him what I did, he didn't say anything. He went to bed, and so did I. I finally slept a good night's sleep.

The next day I went to my class with my arms completely covered, hiding the cuts and stitches. I didn't see nor talk to any of my friends. After class I went home to concentrate on the work I needed to get done for school and to find an apartment. I finally found one two days later and moved in the next Tuesday, within a week of leaving the hospital. I didn't tell any friends and moved only with the help of my mom. I gave no one my address and phone number.

After moving to my new place I concentrated on my schoolwork and began studying more about Hinduism. I called my friend Darren and went out with him a couple of times. After a long time I finally told him about what had happened. He understood, for he had tried to kill himself too. He also had a degree in Psychology, and was my age, not younger like Sarika and my ex-roommate, so we could relate to each other.

It seemed I had finally faced the world. Soon after telling Darren I called my friend Bob. I have known Bob for my entire life. He understood everything and told me I was welcome to come up there and stay with him. I was moving on with my life, yet was still in contact with Sarika. She even stayed the night at my place after I had been there a week. I e-mailed her everyday. I was still in love with her and hoping she would come back to me. I had forgiven her for everything and I prayed and hoped every day. Hope was keeping me going. I began to look within and find myself again.

Finding Myself

After moving into a studio apartment, by myself, I found I had a lot of time on my hands. I would come home from class, do my homework, then read a book. I had no television and no one to spend time with. I felt my friends, or rather those that I hung out with, were gone. So I started to look inwards, toward myself. I began searching the Internet for Hindu teachings. I easily found what I was looking for.

The teachings I found focused on self-realization, so I began to meditate three or four times a day. I especially meditated when I thought of Sarika or was lonely, both of which happened often. I began to see what I had done with Sarika, and the bad habits of daily life that had become routine. I read more from the Internet, and learned more about myself.

I learned how to focus my thoughts. I began to pull myself out of the quagmire I had gotten myself into. I studied and began to focus my energies back into school, where they should have been all along. I began to see me, the way I felt about everything. I let my emotions go, all the anger, lust, and hatred. I peeled away the emotions covering my heart and found the love that had always been there, hidden.

I had a burning desire in my heart to learn more, to learn from someone other than an inanimate object. I searched for a Hindu temple to study at. I wanted to embrace what I felt in my heart, to embrace myself.

I found a temple in Sacramento, California. I decided to go down over Spring Break, and spend a week there studying and praying. Sarika gave me the name Arjuna, I chose Surya Kumar. I decided to change my name to Arjuna Surya Kumar and embrace Hinduism.

I found I truly believed in non-violence, that god was within everyone, and that we are all the same, simply human beings. I began to realize when I felt the way I do about the world and the society of the western world. I noticed how egocentric people around me were, and how materialistic. I began to reject material possessions, even more than I already had. I began to see the beauty in everyday life, the trees, grass, and birds. I realized I wasn't a freak, as I thought when I was

growing up. I realized why I didn't cry or feel sad at funerals.
I realized the person wasn't dead, just their shell of a body was.
It took me a long time to formalize what or who I was.

I also began to realize that maybe I am not going to die,
ever. It sounds weird to say, because I have been so ingrained
with Western thought that everyone dies. I say no one dies,
they just change form, their energy changes. Energy cannot be
created or destroyed. I could finally see that. I still wasn't 100
percent positive about all of this, about anything. I was unsure
about everything. I decided that when I left for Sacramento I
would start out walking and go from there, to make a pilgrimage of sorts. I decided not to plan for anything anymore.
Life would come and go, time was an illusion.

I studied hard for my finals, realized my spirit is intertwined
with the rest of the world and that I had to break the cycle of
running, either from those that hurt me or whenever I felt bad.
I decided to learn more from a Hindu priest and the community
in Sacramento.

Spring Break Journal Introduction

I am in my last terms of college and have been in a continual process of learning. I have looked everywhere for a God and religion. Over the past two years I have primarily looked within, and towards Eastern Religions, specifically Hinduism. Due to a personal tragedy and crisis, I looked further within and more towards Hinduism. Before Spring Break of 1998 I decided to go study and further my knowledge of Hinduism. I wanted to go to a Temple. The closest temple to me was in Sacramento, California. I wanted to embrace what I already knew, learn what I didn't, and answer my insecurities. So I arranged with the Panditji in Sacramento to visit for a week. I planned on walking down as far as I could, then catch the bus from wherever I was the rest of the way. So here is the journal I kept on my journey, or as I call it, my pilgrimage.

The Night Before, 17 MARCH 98

My name is Arjuna Surya Kumar. I was formerly known as Aaron Patrick Falotico. This is the day before I leave for Sacramento, to learn from great teachers.

18 MARCH 98

It's 7:30 am and I am off, leaving Corvallis, OR. I am excited to go. I am just off of Hwy 34, on the railroad tracks headed south. I got a ride from Mr. Misc, a refrigerator repair guy, going to Linn Benton Community College. He's headed to Phoenix. I thought of Sar a couple of times, but I thought of a lot of things a couple of times. I am glad I am alone. I removed my coat, had some water and a banana, I left the peel. I don't know what time it is, but I figure its almost noon. I had to stop to put shorts on, and eat. I'm not quite sure exactly where I'm at but I still have Mary's Peak to my right. I am not sure what, if anything, will happen in Sacramento but I have learned a lot about myself already. I'm off the tracks and headed towards I-5, I'm at American Rd, wherever that is. I will probably catch the bus on Friday. My left knee is hurting pretty badly. So I am resting it more and more. I am not going very fast anymore and am enjoying the slower pace.

19 MARCH 98

I'm in Redding, California. I'm at a 76 truck stop. I've tried paging mom, but it was busy. I went east on American Rd, through Halsey on the way to I-5. I hitched a ride to Creswell with this great old couple and their dog. They had moved to Eugene two years ago and were out for a drive. A little past Creswell, my knee was hurting pretty badly. I caught a ride with a log truck driver, on his way home. We talked about everything from cars to religion. He is married to a Mormon. He dropped me off at Myrtle Creek, 80 miles! A little after Myrtle Creek, I was picked up by an 18-year-old. I suspect, a student at the community college north of Roseburg. He is studying computer science, very shy and reserved. He had a great bumper sticker, "Don't steal, the government doesn't need the competition." He dropped me off at Canyondale. I continued walking; my knee was very sore. I made it to Eugene by 3, Myrtle Creek by 5:30. It started to get dark but I didn't stop. I tried sleeping under an overpass but was too cold. I continued walking; my left knee was swollen. I decided to take the bus Friday. (It was Thursday) I kept walking slowly, would stop for a while to rest, then continue walking. I stopped often, fell asleep for a little while then kept walking. I had no idea of time. As I was walking up a hill or mountain, a semi stopped. I didn't expect it, nor was I hitch-hiking at the time. A guy named Hank just wanted me to keep him awake. It was 2 am. He was awesome. He had been to and in two monasteries. We talked a lot of philosophy and religion. I was amazed because truckers aren't supposed to pick people up; it's against the law. He wants to write a book. It sounds like a good book. We went through inspections just inside California. He stopped at Redding and here I am. It's after 7 am now. My knee is still swollen, and I haven't slept. I am having fun and am farther along than I thought I would be.

I am with God, and have surrendered to him. I have thought of Sar, but still don't miss her. Even when I talk to people I really don't think about her like I used to. Maybe that'll change or I will. No matter what happens I am at peace and love is emanating from me. Well, it's time to get going. Hopefully I have enough money to pay for this meal! They even play country music at the truck stop!

Well I got kicked off the Freeway, so I'm off to the bus station. I hope my GI Bill went through. The CHP kicked me off! It's a little after ten; I'm boarding the bus at 11 and will be in Sacramento around 3. My left knee is still swollen and it hurts to walk. I have a nice sunburn! I still can't get over Hank. He's probably the greatest philosopher I've met yet. He was or is only like 47, but has done many things. MY GI Bill hasn't gone through yet, hopefully by Monday! So my adventure is almost over, I am excited and hopeful to learn about more about Hinduism, the stuff not in books. I will go to the public library and try to e-mail mom and Sar. I kind of miss her, but haven't slept yet so I'm too tired to really feel much. I've been up since a little after 6 yesterday morning. I can't wait to rest; maybe I'll sleep on the bus.

Well, I'm in Sacramento. I slept a little on the bus. Soon I will go to the Hostel. Maybe I'll find the public library first. My knee is sore and I hurt all over. Oh well, I am happy. My adventure is over, and no matter what happens tomorrow I had fun and learned a lot.

It's about 5:45, I'm headed to the Temple. I e-mailed Sar and mom, I can actually use Telnet at the library. I checked into the Hostel. There are two statues of panthers that reminded me of Sar; they are out front of the US Bank building. They are cool, lounging, right next to the library. The hours of the library are odd. I hope to hear from Sar. The Netscape is slow; I must learn patience. I'm waiting for the bus. This has been a good trip so far; I thank God, for being with me, as I surrendered unto him.

It's about 9 p.m., I am tired. I look forward to tomorrow, the next day and the next and so on. I want to learn so much. I was given the idea of learning Hindi! I even got the name of a book. I know so little. The Temple is made up of mostly Indians from Fiji. The Temple is beautiful, so awesome, there are two pictures of Arjuna shooting arrow while Lord Krisna drives the chariot. Well I need to sleep; I am going to read the Gita then go to sleep. I am glad I came and have no worries about anything. Sar was right, my feet are ugly.

20 March 98

I woke up at 5:30. It is a beautiful day. The bus ride is very good, a lot of interesting people. Sacramento is a beautiful city. I didn't notice how beautiful it was last time I was here. I enjoy riding the bus and seeing all of the people who are so busy going and coming. They are all trying to achieve the American Dream. I think even the homeless people are. I'm at the Temple, its 8:05 am. I look forward to learning more. Breakfast was good. I will eat here from now on. I am feeling more and more relaxed. I feel at home. Peace. The Panditji's wife is so nice, a great cook. I hope, if I get married, to marry a woman like her. The Panditji has four kids, one daughter that is married, one son, and two daughters in school. The president of the Temple's name is Vangan. (I am not sure if I spelled that right.) I have been offered a wife, and Indian girl who is the Panditji's brother's daughter. She is in Fiji. I don't know right now. I plan to spend some more time thinking, studying. It would take time to arrange everything and I would have to travel to Fiji. I know I want to finish school before I get married. The Panditji is not a US Citizen, but is a permanent resident alien as a religious worker. I have no idea why we, in this country, need to classify people as resident, non-resident, alien, etc. What is an alien?

An Indian wife would be great! A wedding ceremony is three days long. The last day is the ceremony. The first day is events and rituals, the same with the second. I am at the second day of a wedding. This is a girl party, I have been told. There is a lot of food being prepared. I think everybody here is from Fiji! I am at the house of the bride's mother. The bride is Indian; the groom is Hispanic, white. All of the women here are wearing saris. This is the Kata ceremony. I want to learn to Sanskrit as well. Some Indian women tattoo their husband's names on their right wrist. This is the bride's ceremony. There are strong values in Hinduism, the values dear to me. Family is a big part of everyday life. I like the family central ideology. I wish I had a strong family. I think I will strive to make a strong family. My mom is a strong member of my family. I want to include my brother. It is time to forgive the past and move onto the future. I will love. I do love all of my family and my new family. Marriage is a strong bond between a man and woman, and the two families involved. I was just asked who I was. Everybody here thought I was the bride's husband to be.

It's a little after 3 and we are back at the Temple. We had lunch of asparagus mixed with spices, rice and a different curry from before. Soon I will sit down and ask questions. The ceremony was awesome, so beautiful. I look forward to my own wedding, a Hindu wedding. I also met Armus who is 24, and really cool. I hope to create and maintain a web page for this Temple. I need to get the Vedas, Upanishads and Sutras.

I have had a great day. Reading, talking, and learning. I have helped put addresses on flyers and counted donations. I plan to send money when I get home and have some. I get rides home every night so far. I have been asked again if I want a Hindi wife. I am struck with silence, whenever I am asked or it is mentioned. I am at peace and am learning no longer for myself but of myself, God, Vishnu, Krishna.

Its about 11pm, I'm back at the Hostel. I had dinner and tea at Singh's house. He is very outspoken. He was the founder, or one of them, of the Temple. I am going back to the Temple tomorrow at 9. I am going to help decorate for the wedding and learn. Oh yeah, Singh taught me two things to always re-member: Karma Yoga- to do things with no expectations of benefit, and to judge people on their behavior not birth right.

I thought of Sar quite a bit today. I don't know why. Every time marriage came up or when the children were dancing I re-membered her. What am I going to be like when I get back? My name. I am being addressed as Arjuna now!

I met two little girls today, Panditji's nieces, Hetka and Satchi. They are neat, very buoyant and full of life. I love them and all the people I have met. One girl or woman thought I was a journalist, until I told her it was more personal than that.

21 MARCH 98

Its Saturday about 8:30 am. I'm waiting for the bus. I found out I have no money in my account. I need $170 to stay until Sunday the 20th and buy a bus ticket back. I have faith that all will work out fine. My GI Bill should go through soon. I don't know when. I am looking forward to attending the wedding. I called mom and will call her tomorrow to see if she can help. I feel like I've been here a week already. I have observed and learned so much. Only part of it is written here. It's almost 10:00; I'm at the Mandir. There are chairs set up and a gazebo is on the platform. The banana tree and palm tree from yesterday's ceremony are in the middle of the Gazebo. The banana tree represents or signifies one fruition, one marriage; the palm is strong and bends in strong wind but always comes back to straight. The palm signifies a strong marriage, one that survives the storm. Yellow ribbon is used, because the bride wears yellow, and yellow chalk like dye is used throughout the three days. The trees will be planted at the couple's home. I feel when I get back, whenever that is, I won't want or desire Sar. I will keep in contact with her because she is my friend. I will concentrate on school, and my spirituality. She will always have a place in my heart but not in my life. I don't really miss her or want to see her, even though I do think about her. I don't really want to see her when I get back, I'd rather just e-mail her, and not everyday. I am actually looking forward to getting home and back to school. I may leave Wednesday, Thursday, or Friday. I may be forced to leave, having no money. I need $123 to just stay in the hostel and another $42 or hopefully less for a bus ticket. So the total is $172. Something will come up, I am not worried, or doubting anything, just figuring out the money. I am formulating my fasting, Saturday, Sunday, and Monday. The days I focus the most on spirituality and learning. I will eat only one meal each day, maybe. At least Monday's will be one meal. I can smell rain. It is one of the most beautiful scents in the world.

It's about 2 and the rain is falling after many days of warm weather. The rain is life, brings life and nourishes life. There is nothing that does not need the rain. It, rain, is the epitome of reincarnation. It falls, is absorbed, changes into vapor, rises to the clouds, then falls in the liquid form again, the cycle of life, reincarnation in a nutshell. The Temple holds a maximum occupancy of 750, but there are only enough chairs for less than 400. There are 850 people invited. I don't think they will all show up. The priest who is performing the ceremony is here, and doesn't like the setup. There is quite a bit of politics involved with this Temple, I'm not sure about others. I pray to god, Vishnu, I will be able to stay. Even though I know to find the mantras and have learned by watching, what to do when paying respect to the gods. I am just learning more about the culture. I believe I could fit into the culture if my skin was darker and I could speak Hindi. I've been given the all-important phone to answer, its 6:45, the wedding process has begun. I would be overjoyed if Sar and I were married like this, but I know it will never happen. The Mandir has filled; there are still places to sit though. I like this big wedding. The tradition and values of Hindu life is what I will strive for!

THE WEDDING: The groom, before entering the Temple meets the bride's family and a puja, or prayer is held. The groom is seated in the archway next to the bride's family. Live music and singing is played in the traditional versions. The seating appears to be mixed; the groom is still in the archway with the best man and priest nearby. The bride is not in the Temple yet, its 6:45. The groom has moved to the gazebo, stage. The bride is making her way in to the Temple with her party. Everyone stood as the bride entered. There is an exchange of good wishes. We are actually ahead of time, amazingly, about ten minutes. The bride and groom are sitting while the orchestra plays and sings a song of blessing. This was one of the most beautiful, powerful wedding ceremonies I have ever witnessed. I love the simplicity and rituals that have meant so much for so long.

There is another ceremony after dinner to prepare the couple for their new home. I will not attend it. The whole ceremony signifies and strengthens the institution, for lack of a better word, of marriage. The ceremony flowed like water, and lasted for about an hour or so. But it wasn't stiff, removed, or boring. It was truly enjoyable. I want to attend more. I don't know the couple but feel something in my heart for them and everyone else.

I am truly a Hindu! A Hindu in the heart and spirit, now to become a full Hindu which includes the mind. Maybe next summer I will go to India or Fiji, that way I can learn the culture. I found out today the priest's son's, (I need to remember names) birthday is on the 11th of April as well.

It's about 10:30, I'm back at the Hostel for what could be my last night. I pray to Vishnu that I am able to stay and devote more time to him. If not then hopefully enough time to stay until Wednesday or Thursday. I have learned a lot today, the stories of Ganesh, Shakti and Vishnu, Siva, Rama, and Krishna. I want to learn more stories. I would like to share and learn from Sar. The vows told me that Sar is the one for me, but it is up to her. I know I shouldn't but I have doubts. I don't know, maybe I should accept one of the offers given to me and meet someone else. The people I have met so far are really nice and are kind of amazed or taken back by me wanting to learn Hinduism and become Hindu. A Sihk invited me to their Temple but he didn't seem friendly or nice. I am halfway through the Gita and this book, so maybe I'm halfway through my trip? It really has no effect, good or bad, as far as what happens.

22 MARCH 98

It's about 8:30, I am at the Hostel. I don't know where mom is, but I am here at least one more night and have become a member of International Hostels. So I figure I need $127 to stay until Sunday and buy a bus ticket home. If I leave Wednesday I would need $75, Thursday $88, Friday $101, Saturday $114, Sunday $127, or Tuesday $62, or Monday $49. I could save money with the sooner I buy a ticket with a student discount and 3 days prior to departure. I will soon head out to the Temple. I can't wait to see the dancing. I have formulated my fasting. Saturday I take little or no food or water, Sunday I take water and one meal, Monday I take water and one meal and fruits or chocolate for snacks.

It's 1030 and I am at the Temple. I haven't gotten a hold of mom yet. Arman has taught me a lot yesterday. Sar knew very little about Hinduism, just how to practice. I wish I would have met Arman sooner! I am now watching some girls dance, or learn how. The girls are learning classical dance, from southern India, Madras. I was just taught the puja, which is very interesting. I should come down here for my b-day. If Sar doesn't want to go to Seattle I will come down here. Maybe she will come here with me? I am invited to dinner at the priest's house before I leave, probably Thursday night. To end where I began, a full circle, so $88 is all I need. Nay means no. People find it amazing I fast, especially fasting for three days. Too bad I haven't told anyone I have fasted for 7 days and more.

It's about 4:00 and I finally got a hold of mom, she has a pinched nerve. I have to call her back tonight to figure out what we are going to do with the money situation. Its not like I won't have the money in a week! This is funny! I have only 7 more chapters to read. The priest makes very little money for the hours he works or is at the Temple and family he has. The people of the community should take care of him and his family! I'm being taught Hindi! Too bad for Sar!

Well its about 9:30 I'm back at the Hostel, my last night. I will stay at the priest's house from now until Sunday night when I leave.

23 MARCH 98

It's 12:00; I'm at the Temple. I had breakfast at Denny's with Joel from England. I went and got my ticket at the bus station. I am by myself in the Temple trying to put sentences together in Hindi. Last night I kind of met a very pretty girl and was teased, at least I think, about marrying her. I will probably come down for my birthday, and ask the priest to find me a wife. I don't miss Sar, and kind of want to go to school down here. I don't know when I will be going home. I plan on going to the library tomorrow; I will check the ATM for my check as well. I am not worried. I will go to the library and the bus station to leave Thursday night. I need to solve the mystery of the GI Bill. Plus I don't want to impose too long. I will be back. I am enjoying learning Hindi, maybe at the end of summer I will stay for ten days and just learn Hindi. I will also learn on my own. My knee doesn't hurt much and my sunburn is peeling.

It's about 10:15pm, I'm at Pandit's house. I have a big Hindi-English dictionary. When I get home I will need to rewrite it. I need to memorize all these words. I am beginning to understand more and more of what people are saying. I am being fed food every time I turn around. I don't know when I will go home, I will check my e-mail tomorrow and my ATM. I already know more Hindi than Sar; maybe I will help her learn though probably not. I don't care to be around her, I want to find someone who will love and hopefully marry me. Sar can go somewhere else.

24 MARCH 98

It's 7 a.m., and I slept well. I am peeling like crazy! I am going to the library today, to check my e-mail and grades. My grades probably aren't in until tomorrow. If I still have no money in my account I will leave Thursday night. I need to take care of that. If I do have money I will stay until Sunday.

Well, I don't have any money in my account and I have no idea when I'm going home. I think I should leave Saturday night so I can rest and square things away before I go back to campus. I wrote Sar. I don't miss her. There was something else but I can't remember. I got my grades, oh well about Philosophy. I got a "D" in my third Political Science class as well. The Puja tonight for Lord Rama was awesome. Panditji's mom is ill in Fiji. He surprised me by wishing me the best with my studies.

25 MARCH 98

It's been one week since I left my home. It's 11:00 am; I am at Panditji's sister's house. I'm going to help watch three little girls, Devia, Sakshi, and Heckta. I'm leaving Saturday night; I have so much to do when I get back home. I am being pushed or teased to marry Saleshni from Fiji.

26 MARCH 98

Tonight will be one week since being here. I have finally seen pictures of Saleshni. She is pretty. I was being pressured last night to marry her. I told everyone I would decide in 6 months or so. If she is like Rasheka I probably will, I don't know. I am learning more and more Hindi everyday. I am going home Saturday night. I will work on my web page, and all the other things I need to do. I kind of miss Sar, but not really. I don't know if I even want to see her. I guess I'm "over" her. I know I have found peace and am happy with myself. I have money in my account. I bought a new wallet, some stuff for Sar, and a card for the Sharma's. Panditji gave me $20 last night; I'll give him $320 tomorrow night and $50 to the deities. I e-mailed mom and Sar and Andy. I told Sar and mom I'd be home Sunday. It's been one week since I have been in Sacramento. I have two more days left. I'm kind of excited to go home but sad to leave. I know I will be back. I am peeling my skin off my arms, like a snake. I know I am growing spiritually. I will give Panditji a card either tomorrow or Saturday before I leave, for him to open at home. I don't know. I was just given a book, "Teach Yourself Hindi," from Sakuntha, the girl who gave me a ride back to the Hostel last Thursday. I have come full circle. This is the book I was looking at last Thursday. I actually participated in the puja tonight. I definitely felt something, I don't know what but it was good. My mind is clear and focused. I have a string tied around my wrist and a small red mark on my forehead. I don't know why yet. A favorite drink is Kava, from Fiji and other islands. I have met so many people.

27 MARCH 98

I shaved this morning! This is the first time in about 2-3 weeks. I will give Panditji the card tomorrow, probably just before I leave through someone else, maybe one of his kids or wife. I don't know. I don't feel I have to or should do this, but I want to. I do not need the money and he is my Panditji. I believe in taking care of the Pandit, Temple, community, in that order. I leave tomorrow night at 11:15. Wow what a week!

I talked with Rasheka last night for a while. She is funny. I need to back into exercise and scheduled eating. It's about 9am. I don't miss Sar but I do talk about her because people want to know how I learned Hinduism, then ask about my friend. Too bad her family is the way they are and she is the way she is. Oh well, what goes around comes around - karma!

28 MARCH 98

My last day here in Sacramento. Yesterday was a quiet, peaceful day. I didn't go to the Mandir. It's about 8:30, I will go to an ATM then to the Mandir until about 9:30 tonight to catch the bus downtown to the Greyhound station. It is the beginning of Ramayan.

It's 10:30 a.m. and I'm at the Mandir. Panditji is set up in front of a deity with the symbol for the sun in front of him. It's in rice. I have been given two shirts, a towel, and a watch from Panditji and his family. The puja was good. I don't know why but I am not thinking of anything really. I feel out of it right now. I'm neither happy nor sad. I am thinking about four or five steps behind. I am also reflecting on the past week and am apprehensive about seeing Sar. I don't really want to but my heart says yes and no. I don't know. I don't feel like I love her, not saying I didn't, I just don't anymore. She can do whatever, she is not what she was and I don't want to be around her. I am happy, peaceful and content with my life and who I am. I don't want to have anyone disturb that. I just cut the grass. It's been a long time since I've cut the grass anywhere. I'm still not thinking, it's more like contemplating.

It's 1:42. I'm glad this day is not going slowly or quickly. A separate stage has been set up for Ramayan.

It's about 5:30 p.m., and it's raining. I've talked to a girl, I have no idea what her name is but she is 20 and very pretty. The puja is the same as Tuesday, except there are a lot more people here. Panditji gave me some sandalwood beads and some incense.

It's 8 p.m., 1-1/2 hours.

29 MARCH 98

It's 12:47 a.m., and I'm at the bus station waiting for another bus. All the others are full and left. The puja and music that followed were cool. I didn't want to say good-bye, or leave. I gave my address and phone number to Yogi, I think that's her name. I don't think she'll write. Well it's about 1:00 a.m. and I'm on the bus. We'll leave soon hopefully.

It's almost 8:30 and I'm south of Roseburg. I've thought about Yogi almost all night long. I don't know why. I am feeling apprehensive about seeing Sar. I don't really want to. I want to go back and talk with Yogi. Weird! How can you really meet someone just as you are leaving? I have met so many nice people on this trip. I was given food for the trip home. I'll eat it for dinner tonight.

10 APRIL 98

It's about 7:00 p.m. I feel bad because I have hurt the woman I love and she says she no longer loves me. I have never felt this way about anyone in my life, with the exceptions of my best friends. And I considered her my best friend. I have forgiven her for hurting me. I am alone. I am not happy nor sad, just numb. I feel nothing. Maybe I will write more to-morrow. I'll be 26 tomorrow.

11 APRIL 98

Happy Birthday to me! I feel like I have come full circle, since coming to this fine learning institution. I came here and lived by myself and am doing it again. Concentrating on my studies. The last year has been one of the best I've ever had, if not the best.

I feel the internal struggle I've been going through for the last two months has come to an end. It actually started at the beginning of winter term, but then progressed. I went from the highest of highs to the lowest of lows. I did things that I can't believe I did, some were logical, some illogical, and some bordered on the psychotic. My emotional state would fluctuate so badly I didn't know who I was or what I was doing. I regret doing some things, others I don't. I am finally comfortable. The important part is I feel good about me. In the fall I will graduate, two years and one term since coming here. Pretty amazing! It can be done. Even with going through a rough time. Happy Birthday, Arjuna!

12 APRIL 98

Well, it was a typical birthday; no one called. Reconciliation and forgiveness, these two things are important. In order to find happiness and the love that is within. So long for now.

A Week of Hell

The day after my twenty-sixth birthday I went over to Darren's and got drunk. I was stressed from all the reading and writing I had to do for an assignment in a class that was repetitive. I also felt like hell from hearing that the one person I loved more than anything in the world did not love me. I decided to drown my sorrows in alcohol, to obliterate everything that was going on in my life and the world around me.

I got home around eleven and tried to call Sarika, no answer. I called the guy she was seeing. She was there. She had lied to me; she told me there would be no more guys in her life for a long time, which was another crushing blow. The guy yelled at me. I told him that if he wanted to settle it we could settle it the way he wanted. He wanted to fight. He hung up on me so I called back, again and again. He told me he called the cops. Once again a great depression came over me, as reality hit. All I wanted was the woman I loved. She had just said the week before that she did love me. How can someone just drop an emotion like love that fast? I was confused.

I left to go to the store. I bought M&M's and some rat poison. When I got home I started a bath, and put some of the poison in a beer and began to drink it. Soon after there was a knock on the door, as I went to answer it I put on my robe to cover my naked body and the cut I began on my wrist. I was handed a summons to appear in court for telephonic harassment. Once again devastation reigned supreme! I drained the tub, sat in front of my computer and puked up the beer, poison, and pizza. I swept everything into the trash and went to bed.

The next day I woke up and didn't feel like doing anything. I felt like leaving, running away, while thoughts raced through my brain. Every thought that entered my mind was of her, or came back to her. The pain she caused me, the good times we had. The love I felt. The love she gave me. I was depressed. I finished off the poison, and went to the store to buy something more powerful. I bought some drain cleaning lye. When I got home I drew a bath, and got in. I began to cut my wrist. The

blood flowed with little puffs, into the water. As I watched the
blood flow, I felt the love for her go with it, or at least tried. I
was tired and the blood flow stopped. I got out of the tub and
took a little bit of the drain cleaner. Nothing happened. I felt
fine considering all the stuff in my body and the amount of
blood that I had lost. I didn't eat anything; instead I took a
bigger dose of the drain cleaner. A great burning erupted im-
mediately from the back of my mouth and throat. I drank as
much water as I could. Then I fell asleep.

I woke up about an hour later and felt fine, except it was
hard to swallow. I only thought of her and relieving the pain of
the gut wrenching loss she put me through. My world of
harmony collapsed because of what she did to me, but I still
loved her. I wanted her to feel the pain of losing something so
close to you, like I felt. I took the rest of the aspirin that was in
my house, over a hundred tablets, and drank a beer. I lay
down, tired. My stomach started churning. I tried to get comfortable and finally fell asleep again. When I woke I grabbed
the trashcan and puked white syrup made of the aspirin into it.
I went back to sleep. I woke a little while later but didn't
move. The world around me spun, everything was spinning.

My body was spiraling down, out of control. The colors of
the day were blending. Bright sparks of light flashed as I spun.
Brown, White, Green, FLASH, Brown, Blue, Red, FLASH,
Brown, Yellow, FLASH, Brown, Black, FLASH, Black,
FLASH, Black, Black, Darkness. The light of day and life was
gone, only darkness remained, but I was still breathing, feeling.
I was falling down; I felt the rush of world and my material
possessions passing by. Whoosh! There went the computer.
Whoosh! I didn't know what that was. I awoke out of a dark
pit, with a jump, my mind racing. My thoughts only of her, I
didn't leave my house that day until after dark to check my
mail. I skipped class.

The next sunshine, I didn't know what day it was. When I
woke up I went straight into the bathroom to take a bath and
continue what had become the ritual attempt at death I had
started. After about an hour I gave up again and went in to lie
down. I lay there asking, whoever would listen, to leave the
pain behind and to forget the love I felt. I began to dream, half
conscious.

In the dream I came upon a great river. It was too wide to cross. I stared out across the expanse looking for a way to get across or around it. I sat for a moment then froze completely, after hearing a low growl come from behind me. I turned slowly. Nothing was there but vegetation. Huge leaves blocked my view. I slowly made my way to where the noise came from. All of a sudden the foliage opened and I was face to face with a lion. We looked at each other, then turned upriver and began walking together. We traveled for a long time, wandering the land. Passing through mountain passes, deserts, forests, and through rain, snow, and sunshine we slept together, walked, and hunted together. Then the earth and lion disappeared, and a huge panther face came into focus, winked with bright yellow eyes. The panther was smiling, as it faded away. Next, a kaleidoscope of colors entered my realm, soon followed by a man in a dark suit. He was Death, I presumed. But he did nothing, just stood there. When I finally woke it was late afternoon, by the sun's position.

I was determined to leave this world. I ate nothing, and drank very little. I lay in my bed thinking of her, wondering why and asking myself what did I do to deserve this. I gave her all of me, and she ripped my heart out and laughed. I wanted it all to go away.

The next few days blended together with the previous days, never ending, one becoming the other, and all becoming one. I never left my apartment for any reason. I called no one. I e-mailed my mom and lied to her, telling her everything was all right, and that I was studying hard. In actuality, I didn't go to class. I checked my mail only after dark. I thought constantly of running away, jumping off a bridge, leaving the area, doing something to get away, and leaving everything behind. I thought of the woman I loved. Why was I so hung up on her? I thought of love. How love can be so cruel, so deadly, and yet so beautiful.

I dreamt of her and of her paintings. I was at a gallery, an art gallery; her paintings were hung all around. I was part of the crowd but someone important at the gallery. I was wearing black. She was radiating beauty and talking about her art, her work, to a crowd surrounding her. I was happy, busy talking to a reporter, and watching her. I was on cloud nine. She made her dream come true. She was selling her works. I was in the shadows, quietly supporting her. Silently loving her. Feeling all the emotions the paintings represented. Death, horror, heartache, love. The paintings were gothic, dark, every stroke, an emotion, as if she were painting my emotions, my feelings. It was me in the art. She had painted me. Some how she had tapped into my inner self and presented my life on canvas. That's why I was happy. I woke up hugging her.

As I came fully awake, I realized that I was still in the world of torment, and she wasn't there. My mind drifted rapidly from one thought to another. Different personalities and their voices filled my memory. First there was a child's voice reminding me of the great times I had growing up, playing, without a care in the world. Next came a girl's voice telling me of all the girls I used and the hearts I broke, that I deserved what I got. She said, "What comes around goes around." Finally a man's voice came but said something I couldn't understand. I was half conscious, with my emotions running wild.

First I felt despair, then love, then hatred and finally anger. I grabbed my tie, put it around my neck and tied it to my bed. I cinched it up tight and moved as far away as I could. I began to lose consciousness, and Death reappeared. I asked for him to take me, but he didn't. He just stood there, watching, then left. The world was spinning. I could smell the awful odor coming from my body. The stench of the apartment permeated everything. The dried puke on the floor, the dried blood in the tub, the sweat on the blankets blended into an atrocious smell. I was nauseated. The ache in my stomach from no food, only beer and M&M's, grabbed me from my toes.

A week had passed and I was starving, dehydrated, and weak. As I lay on the bed just about out of it, strangling myself, the phone rang. I didn't get up to answer it. The answering machine picked it up. It was my best friend Bob and his daughter Mariah. Hearing Mariah's voice, asking for her Uncle woke something inside of me. After they hung up I jumped up, cooked and ate some eggs and potatoes. I called my mom, and asked her to come get me. She said she would about one in the morning. Then I packed and cleaned the apartment as best I could. I Sprayed air freshener everywhere I could, and as I waited I began to organize what I wanted to take and what I wanted to get rid of. The things Sarika had given me were thrown away.

After organizing and packing I went over to Darren's to tell him I was dropping out of school and moving to my mom's to collect myself. Later that night my mom came and got me. That day I began my road to recovery, to heal my wounds, inside and out, emotional and physical.

Emotional Strain

A gurgling resonates from the pit of my stomach. Darkness falls over my body. Hate. Anger. Revenge fills my every thought. I sit there not knowing me. Who am I? What am I? I am a monster. I feel the knife sliding into my back, placed there by the one I love. The blood, darkened, black, flows freely down my spine. The once brightness that filled my days, is now filled with doom and gloom. The reaper himself is present at every turn, every conscience moment. Death lurks. Betrayal brings the darkness. Revenge and hatred fill the air. The putrid smell of anger is everywhere. The smell fills my nostrils. Darkness has befallen the light. What light? The black flows from my back, creating a deep pool at my feet. Death watches over, monitoring the progress of the anger. I am alone with failure all around me. There is no love to save me. There is nothing, no hope. Dreams are dashed like a ship on a rocky shore. Betrayal. Why? I don't have the answer. I just deal with the aftermath, and the darkness.

You

You grew up in a sheltered family, protected from the world. You weren't allowed to have a boyfriend, let alone date. You were sent to school, first time away from home, to study. You weren't looking for a relationship. Your parents ruled your life, along with your religious beliefs. You stayed to yourself. Studied hard. You lived as you were supposed to, as you believed. Then you met me.

We just started to hang out, talk, and study. You wanted a friend and you found one. You found a friend for life just like you wanted. I heard about your life, your parents. I envied you, how you grew up, with a loving family. I wanted that for my family, I want that for my family.

I was your first kiss. Your best friend. You trusted me, believed in me. You were having fun, and falling in love. You loved me. I could feel it. So could you. I was your first, for everything. You were my last. You told me everything; you gave me your all. You were you, and I didn't want to change that. You didn't want to change me; I loved you for that. You were happy. You were in love.

You told me that I was the best person you ever met. You told me I was your best friend. You told me I would do anything for you, I would You told me you would do anything for me. You told me you loved me. You told me we would be together forever, at least as friends. You were wonderful.

You would reassure me, hold my hand. You wanted to be around me. You would laugh at my jokes. You taught me so much. You loved me. I loved you. I still do.

Me

I grew up in a broken home. There were step families on both sides and moving from one house to another, living from month to month. Surrounded by friends, real and imaginary, my family struggled to survive. Government assistance was part of the struggle. I didn't know what a loving family was. I only knew divorce and single mothers and my friends were all the same. I grew up playing and living sports, having fun and not caring about much. Living life on the streets of a small town, the streets of reality. My life was not extremely hard but not sheltered in any way. I saw life as it's lived from the other side, the side people don't want to see.

I grew up seeing my brother beaten by my grandmother, while she told me not to cry. I buried my tears, then buried my emotions. I felt loss at an early age when my aunt passed away at a young age in a tragic car accident. Death was with me ever since, family members dying every year. Grief was not an emotion I shared. I only shared joy and happiness. I grew up not in books but in life.

I worked through high school and paid my own way through college. I had to earn money to go to college. No one paid for me. I had to pay my own way, all the time. Mommy and Daddy weren't there for me.

I was your first love. I loved you more than anything. I dreamed of you, a long time before I ever met you. You completed me, made me whole. I promised myself to you. I promised I would love no other. I promised myself you would be the last. I had been hurt before. I promised never again.

I loved you more than anything. Though I was strong willed, emotionally and spiritually strong, I had walls, emotional barricades, that no one could penetrate. I let you in to my fortress. I told you my dreams and let you see my emotions. I opened up, I promised I wouldn't. I loved you.

Silhouette

You were standing there, a silhouette in my world. You were a permanent fixture on my island of reality. I still see you there sometimes, but faintly and not real. You were warm, caring, loving, and joyous. Now there is sadness, and darkness has fallen across the landscape. The sun has set. The barren hills are scarred, where beauty, joy and happiness once reigned. Two people who loved each other more that anything else. Two souls intertwined in the barren, scarred hills. Two people destiny brought together, who knows what ripped them apart. The only signs left are the scars on the hills. There is barren wasteland where beauty once lived. Someday joy, beauty, happiness, and love may grow again where desolation is today. Two destined lovers. Two destined souls. Who knows?

There she is standing on my island. Who let her on? Love did. Here silhouette in my world, her shadow is all that remains. I will love that shadow forever, as I promised her silhouette.

Is that love?

Everywhere I go a song is playing in my head. One song in particular repeats itself, with the lyrics: "Is this love? I want you to show me."

I know love.
I have loved, I was loved.
I was there once.
I still feel it today.
As far as the future goes, I don't know.
The future. What is in store?
Love. I doubt it.
I was her first, she was my last.
She broke my heart, but I still love her.
She told me to forget about her.
I am trying.
But she is still in my head.
Still there playing.
Everything is still there.
As if it happened yesterday.
I seek refuge from her, but I cannot get away.
She made my knees buckle every time I saw her.

My tongue was in knots.
I could not tell her anything coherently.
I would sit there in silence hoping,
she could feel what I felt for her.
I could not express myself.
IS that love?
I don't know, but I liked how it felt.
I liked how it felt.
Now my days are empty.
Am I alone?
I am alone.
My nights are long, dreams filled with her.
IS that love?
I don't know.
Will someone show me?
She was my last,
I don't want to be hurt again.
I don't want to,
I won't let it happen.
I loved her,
I still do.

Is that love?

Open Letter to a Love

Dear love,

I think of you often and wish you were here. I will forget how we parted, but remember how we met and grew together. I will remember the first time you said hello to me. I will remember our first talk. I will remember our first kiss. I will remember your smile. The warmth you brought to my life. The joy you brought to my heart. You made me whole, no longer just a part. I believed I could conquer the world, with you by my side. I remember receiving your letters or e-mails, how excited I was. I will remember your laugh. I joy in making you laugh. I would have done anything for you. I will remember your friendship. I wish I could express how I truly feel my love. But I cannot find the words that express my feelings for you. I will remember you.... for everything good that you are!

One day our paths will cross again, our love will be rekindled and burn on forever. For now my memories of you will fade with time, but my love will never die. You lit a fire in me that is brighter than the sun. You were the sunshine in my life. You were my punkarella. You were my world. I only look forward to the day we reunite. I wish you all the best and remember me for eternity. I believe in you and your love for me. Let that love be your guiding light. Follow that light to the ends of the earth. I will miss you until then. There is only one of you and you are the one I love, let this remind you of your beloved.

No matter what happens, no matter what time of day or year I will be there for you. I want you to remember me for the good times we had and the joy the laughter I brought into your life. I will always remember the way you would listen to me no matter what I said. I will remember the talks we had. I will miss you and welcome you back with open arms. You are my best friend.

Love, Me

Remember

Do you remember me as I remember you? Do you remember the fun times we had? The slap fighting or wrestling. We would be playing one minute and then, in the next, on our way out the door to find something else to do. Do you remember how we would talk about holding each other forever. There were the movies we saw and the letters we would write when you were so far away. Do you remember the promises made?

I remember them all, like it was yesterday. The memories are etched in my mind forever. I can never forget the feelings of joy that came over me when I heard your voice after a long stressful day. I remember just sitting watching you, doing whatever.

I remember how easily you could put me at ease with just your presence.

I fought it all the way. I didn't want to get involved. I even told you it was over, but you convinced me not to. The hold you had and still have on me. I looked beyond your physical attributes and saw the person within. I fell in love with her. Our souls united. We could finish each other's sentences, and thoughts. You knew me better that I knew myself. I still fought it. I didn't want to believe I could be falling in love. You told me your inner thoughts and secrets. I told you mine. We became friends first, best friends, just like everybody says it should be.

Everyone around us envied us. They didn't like the fact we could just laugh at nothing, at each other, and ourselves. The envied how we would do anything for each other, and usually did. We would take a walk in the park, or around campus and we never grew tired of each other's company. The happiness we gave each other, the love we shared I cannot forget.

I remember now, but my memory will fade with age. My love still burns within me, as I bury it beneath a wall, a shield from pain. I promise you and me that I will not get hurt again. I hope.

Hello

Hello, is there anybody out there? I wonder because I get no response. I don't hear your voice anymore. I miss your sweet voice, caresses, and tender kisses. God, what did I do to deserve this? I am sorry. Are you out there? Do you remember me? I love you. Do you love me? I remember everything. Hello my friend. I miss you. It seems so long since the last time we talked. How are you? I am fine. I am living one day at a time. Is there anything I can do? God, are you out there? I am still here, loving you. Loving me. What did I do to deserve this? I miss you. I love you. Love me.

Is there somewhere we can talk? Privately. You were meant for me. We were destiny. I cannot forget you. I can forgive. I am still here. I always will be. I am strong. I am doing what I said I would. I am keeping my promises. Are you? I will be everything I said I would be. Will you? I am here for you. Talk to me.

Peacock Feather

Here is a peacock feather. As I walked along the trail, in the mountainous region of the island. I spotted some tracks. I was looking for wildlife of any kind and this was proof there was. I followed the tiny tracks for a while, not knowing exactly what to expect. Creeping along the forest floor quietly, I peered over a small rise. To my excitement I saw three peacocks. I stopped in my tracks and took out my binoculars. I lay there watching the birds eat. A little while later a noise came from behind me, human. The birds heard it too. In an instant they took off. As they did a feather fell free and drifted softly to the earth. I got up and retrieved the feather, for a reminder of the experience. Now I give it to you. Here is a peacock feather.

Two Stories From a Kid's Perspective

The Day I Received Three Thousand Dollars

One summer I was bored. I just walked around doing nothing. Then one of my neighbors came up to my door and gave me THREE THOUSAND DOLLARS.

I said, "Thanks, but I don't need it."

He said, " Yes you do, go on vacation. I'm getting tired of you walking around doing nothing. Go to New York or Texas, go anywhere you want. As long as you're not bored."

I thought he was trying to get rid of me but he was right. So I took the money and went to Japan. I had fun there because I got to eat Japanese food and see all kinds of Japanese stuff. Then my trip was over, so I went back to my boring house and back to my boring self.

The New Mobile House

The all new Mobile House is ready. It comes in a brief case. All you have to do is press a button, and it turns into a house. It comes in all different colors, red, blue, green, white, or brown. Once you find a good place for a house, what you have to do is build one. Or you can come down to one of the Mobile House's housing ware stores and buy yourself a Mobile House that only costs $24.50 a piece. Or if you like the outside of one of their houses and not the inside, then you can buy one that is the same on the outside, but different than ours on the inside.

My Island

I stood there at the shore of Puget Sound, staring out at the ships, sailboats, and ferries moving about the water. I had been here only a few years before doing the same thing, for a different reason. Back then I was lost in the idea of being there. Now I am trying to find something, and forget something else. I couldn't do either. I just stared, taking in the beauty. My thoughts drifted, then focused on an island, just south of where I was. I remembered the island, a Native Sacred ground. I had been there once, only into the harbor. I remember the tranquility, the beauty. I remember saying to myself that someday I will live on an island like this. I created the island within me. It was hard to get to, hard to conquer. I lived on that island for many years, the island within me. No one came near. I lived in peace, harmony, and tranquility.

That's what I'm looking for now and I cannot find it. I let someone onto my island, she conquered it, and we lived in peace, harmony, and beauty. Then she destroyed it. As I stare out at the Sound I search for another island. Someday I will have another island. I am searching for my island.

What I Learned

After trying to die and missing a week of school I had to go and face the world and get on with life. I wore a coat all the time to cover up the scars. I refused to talk about what happened or where I was for a week. Until I talked to Darren. Darren was the one person who lived near me who didn't leave after I got out of the hospital. He didn't leave because he had been where I was. We talked about everything.

I didn't talk to people in class and left as soon as class was over. All I did was go to class and then straight home. I was trying to find myself and didn't need or want the distractions.

I felt embarrassed for trying to kill myself. I was stronger than that. I was taken over by emotion and the terrible empty feeling within me. I was extremely depressed and didn't see the signs until they were upon me. Humans are fragile, and emotions and feelings cannot be trampled upon. I felt like idiotic and used. How could I have been so foolish? I had promised to protect myself from ever being hurt or used and I failed.

Even though I was furious, I loved her. I should have been angry, but instead I forgave her. My love for her saw past everything, and saw the good in her that was still there. I believed she was being duped into something she said before she wouldn't do. I still believed in her. She had turned her back on love for lust and sex, something I have a hard time believing anybody would do.

Love and happiness is what everyone strives for but when they find it, society tells them there is something better out there. So they abandon love in order to search for something better, only they don't find that better thing. To me nothing compares to love and what love brings to the individual, or the couple.

Psychiatrist and Drugs

I don't believe in psychiatrists or drugs in order to heal the mind. However they are needed for some people in America that have been pushed so far from society and caring people that they have fallen off the edge of what is sane, or the societal norm. There is a way to prevent these people and many others from crossing that line. The answer is very simple - caring.

What most people need is someone who cares, to talk to, to listen, and interact. Caring people would prevent many people from even coming close to the edge, let alone falling off. Instead, psychiatrists prescribe anti depressants and other medications as if they were aspirin. Drugs are not the answer. Dependency on a chemical for emotional balance is wrong. Early intervention and sincerity, in other words, true emotional caring, is the answer.

Caring involves listening, not hearing, and interaction, not reaction. Psychiatrists do not present themselves as caring, really caring. They hear their patients but they don't listen. They also don't interact and reassure their patients that they can get through whatever is troubling them. Their motivation is wrong. Money and self are the wrong motivations.

Caring is motivated by love, definitely not money. In my dealings with psychiatrists they did not present themselves as caring or loving. They treated me as another number, a nothing. They don't have the motivation, the correct motivation, love for their patients, which comes from love for all people.

Where am I now?

These stories and pages tell of a sad and lonely tale. However my entire life has not been a sad tale. There were and are moments of utter joy and happiness. Some times are better than others. This experience has filled me with questions, and some emotions hit me harder than others. An emotional loss and shock to the system is tremendous. I don't recommend it for anyone. I still believe in treating everyone with honesty, respect and open communication. There is nothing better "out there" than what I have "in here," in my heart and soul. I have found love and feel great about it. I love myself.

Still I always ask myself questions. My biggest unanswered questions are these: Where am I now? Why did this happen to me?

Where am I now? That's a good question, because I am not sure. I know I am still here, breathing, alive. I am still confused as hell, taking it one day and sometimes one hour at a time. I struggle every step of the way. I have many questions, still unanswered, and many emotional scars that are still healing. I've tried self-help books, but they didn't help or tell me anything I didn't already know or assume. I have taken everything that she ever gave me and threw it out, I moved away from where she is, to avoid seeing her, and am trying to gather the remnants of my life together and move on.

After this whole episode in my life started, a few months ago, I asked one question that has not been full answered. Why? Why? Why me? What did I do to deserve this? I have done a lot of awful things in my past, but I was "young, dumb, and full of cum" as the old saying goes. I didn't treat people very nicely and was angry all the time. I blamed myself for her doing what she did, leaving me. I could have lived with breaking up then having her find someone else, but not her screwing someone then breakup with me. Hell she wasn't even going to tell me for a few weeks. So I ask why? I treated the one I love like a queen. I did everything she wanted me to do. I stood by her when she went home for four months. Even though I had plenty of opportunities to leave the relationship. I loved her more than anything in the world. I would have done anything for her. I promised her I would never forget her, and that I would always be there for her. I will, I am.

My emotions, love especially, took over my entire thought process. I was devastated, betrayed, crushed and severely depressed. My rational thought process was destroyed and my heart broken. We were together for over a year. We were as close as two people could be. It is extremely hard to just quit something cold turkey. Just ask someone who has tried to quit smoking. Most people turn to a replacement. However I feel there is no replacement for love, or for that matter any emotion.

I didn't know what to do. I did things and said things I didn't mean to do or say

I have come up with an analogy. I loved to play soccer. I played for thirteen years while growing up. I also loved to watch soccer. However when I joined the military my window of continuing to play was closed, and with it my love for the game. Now, I have a hard time watching soccer because I feel I should still be out there playing. I find this to be true with Sarika. I have a hard time even being anywhere near her of anything that reminds me of her, because I feel I should still be with her, I still love her.

I find music to be a release for me, as well as writing. But those are two things I loved before I met her, and nobody can take them away from me. I will always write and listen to music. So now all I have to do is "get over" Sarika, if that is possible.

I don't believe anyone "gets over" anything. The key is not to dwell on the loss; it may seem to be the end of the world, but its not. I feel weird saying that because that's not how I treated it, I dwelled on it. I wanted to lash out at something and somebody, but being non-violent in nature, I couldn't. So instead I lashed out at myself.

Violence is not the answer to anything. Violence and anger have not accomplished anything good for humanity. Instead of violence, communication is the key to everything. People sharing their ideas, thoughts, and emotions would be ideal. But that isn't going to happen anytime soon, because too many people don't have open minds. They are like I was and keep everything bottled up inside and then one day just explode because they feel there is no one to talk to. How many marriages and relationships fail because people can't talk or listen to one another?

Western society, says that lust, sex, money and power are the only things to strive for. Wrong! Anyone who has experienced love, true love and understanding, knows that love is more powerful than anything else in the world.

Now back to a question. How do I feel about Sarika? I can honestly say that I love her. I still feel that. I believe I always will, but that doesn't mean I won't love another. Each person is different. Have I forgiven her? Yes. The reason I can forgive her is because I love her.

The question of will I ever take her back keeps popping into my head. I would say yes, but there would have to be a lot of talking and gradual trust building. I don't see that ever happening, so I am still out there looking. I am looking for the woman who can trust and believe in me as much as I will her. I am still looking. I am still talking.

On The Path

With my soul torn, tattered and ripped, blowing in the breeze, I head down the path of recovery. In the beginning the path was slippery, and my soul acted like a sail in the wind, trying to push me off the path.

Every step is a struggle, one step at a time. There are lessons learned, memories forgotten, and growing up all over again. Questions are asked, few are answered, but somehow faith is restored.

I look back now and realize how stupid I was to try to take my own life. But I then think of the state of mind I was in. I was forced into it. My life was turned upside down, the person closest to me, who I loved and who loved me, betrayed me and felt nothing for doing so. I was pushed to the edge with a breakdown of communication between Sarika and I, then kicked over the edge with her betrayal of my trust. With my thoughts and life around me collapsing I could no longer think rationally about anything. I wondered how anyone could live in this world where people treat each other like this, with no remorse, in such a cold, callous and uncaring way. Every time I thought or tried to think of something my mind would come back to the woman who betrayed me, and then had no remorse for what she did. I fell, and rather than lashing out at anyone or anything, I lashed out at myself.

I should have turned to someone, but whom? My world, my best friend, my sanctuary was destroyed. How could I trust anyone else? There was no one who cared or seemed to care around me. No one asked me what was wrong. No one was paying attention or cared about me enough to ask if everything was all right or if they could help.

The lessons I learned in the one experience are enough to fill an entire lifetime. Treating people with respect. Do not lie. When you hurt other people you hurt yourself, when you hurt yourself you hurt other people. CARE. Care about yourself and care about others.

The most important thing between two people is communication and trust. Breaking the trust between two people breaks down the entire relationship. It destroys the individual whose trust was betrayed.

The betrayal of trust is the beginning of the deterioration of the psyche of soul. Communication can repair the damage or send the person into total breakdown. The breakdown of communication is a key sign to the inner destruction of the soul or psyche. However good communication or just plain talking can help anyone and everyone.

I am confused about who I am and what it is in life I am looking for. I'm confused because everything I was or thought I was, was destroyed by betrayal. How can I trust anyone? If I can't trust anyone then I lose my own security. Without my personal security I cannot give of myself and must stay on the constant defensive. This leads me to be confused and indecisive about everything and everybody.

Some days I live in a shell, hiding from the world. I am riddled with shame and guilt for trying to take my own life because every religion and society looks down upon those that attempt suicide. However suicide is a cry for help, something is wrong, and is not wonderfully cured in a few weeks. There is rage within that needs to be released and a human that needs to be nurtured and cared about. We all make mistakes, and those that attempt suicide are victims. They are victims of a society that no longer cares, and of the people who betrayed them.

I live believing everybody can see my shame and what I did. I fear that people will shun me and not understand. How can someone understand unless they have been there? I live not trusting anyone, not believing anything. I was headed down a path and before I got to the end I was derailed. So now my question is whether of not I should try that path again or search for a new one. The repercussions of my actions are still hitting me and will continue hitting me for the rest of my life. Even now, I try to forget what happened and go on with rebuilding my life but cannot. I find it hard because whenever I look at my wrists and see the scars, all the emotions, and all the thoughts surrounding Sarika and my attempt to kill myself, rush over me again.

Where do I go from here? How can I ever love again?

I had always protected myself against being hurt, or at least thought I did. I stuck to myself, never revealing too much of myself to anyone. Keeping my inner sanctuary secure and safe, I did not even confess who I was to God. I now wear my heart on my sleeve. The walls I built around me crumbled, torn down systematically. I don't think I want to rebuild them. I am able to show my emotions, and am not afraid to. However, I am afraid to trust anyone again. That may fade in time.I am hopefully on the road to recovery. I have been a casualty of love, but I will recover.

It took an attempt to take my own life to realize that there truly is a God or something more powerful than human life. Something saved me, not just once but on several occasions. There is something more powerful than man.

I have studied many religions and even questioned the existence of God. But I am now on the path of enlightenment and the path to self-realization. I was lucky I didn't die. Now, maybe, I'll be able to save someone else's life.

SITTING IN THE GREY

by Vynnette Frederick

I'm sitting in the grey,
Looking out to sea.
Wondering about anything,
As my thoughts run helter-skelter.

I'm sitting in the grey,
Looking out to sea
as the waves break
softly.
I look into the innocent trusting eyes
of a child,
Whose simple pleasure,
is to throw stones into the calm bluish
water,
As my thoughts run helter-skelter.

I'm sitting in the grey,
Looking out onto the horizon.
I look at the child,
running wild,
As I reminisce.

For life and I were never like this.
I stay.
On that solemn day.
Sitting in the grey.